Praise for *Moon on the Meadow*

I love these tactile, quiet, loud, human, heartfelt, musical poems of Pia Taavila. They are not burdened by history or love, but are the essence of both; they don't preach, they just sing to the soul. Pia's artistry is paramount.

—RANDALL KENAN, Author of *Let the Dead Bury Their Dead* and *The Fire This Time*

Pia Taavila is an outstanding ballad singer and scholar of traditional music as well as a poet, and her poems are testimony to her love of music and her passion for words that touch others, and her humanity. For many years Pia has taught writing and literature to deaf students at Gallaudet University, and the poems of *Moon on the Meadow* are witness to her special gift for making words on the page sing out and celebrate both struggles and victories, the joy of communication and community.

—ROBERT MORGAN, Author of *Gap Creek* and *Boone: A Biography*

Through these tender yet sly poems as visually unforgettable as Van Gogh's paintings, Taavila proves to be a master of the painterly gaze on not only what it means to live as a hearing daughter of Deaf parents, but also what it means to yearn for a stronger connection with others of—and outside—her blood. It is this very longing that brings us closer to what she's whispering with her hands, tumbling out there onto the darkened page like a candle's wick catching flame. Her poems "see."

—RAYMOND LUCZAK, Author of *St. Michael's Fall* and *This Way to the Acorns*

With *Moon on the Meadow*, Pia Taavila arrives as a fully grown phenomenon. Her feelingful, moving poems show us the world in vivid detail, as few other poets' do. Surely hers is one of the freshest and most memorable contemporary poetry books of this or any year.

—X. J. KENNEDY, Author of *The Lords of Misrule* and *In a Prominent Bar in Secaucus*

Late in this memorable collection of a life's work, Pia Taavila writes, "Let me live just long enough/to cut and reap my former sorrows." We are fortunate, indeed, that she has done just that—and with time to spare! *Moon on the Meadow* would be a joy to read if it only had the little narratives of her childhood growing up as the hearing child of deaf adults. But Taavila goes on from those poems to an exploration of the larger world, where she succeeds at keeping her imagination open to the possibilities of the luminous moments that present themselves to her. She reminds us that these moments are available to all of us.

—KEITH TAYLOR, Director of Creative Writing Programs at the University of Michigan and of the Bear River Writers' Conference, held annually at Walloon Lake, Michigan

Moon on the Meadow

Moon on the Meadow

COLLECTED POEMS

Pia Taavila

Gallaudet University Press
Washington, DC

Gallaudet University Press
Washington, DC 20002
http://gupress.gallaudet.edu

Library of Congress Cataloging-in-Publication Data

Taavila, Pia.
   Moon on the meadow : collected poems / Pia Taavila.
      p.   cm.
ISBN 978-1-56368-364-0 (alk. paper)
1. Deaf parents—Poetry. I. Title.
PS3620.A23M66 2008
811'.6—dc22

                                    2007040228

Cover painting by Rachel Walters.
Cover and interior design by Dennis Anderson

This collection of poems is lovingly dedicated to

my children and grandchildren:

may you grow straight and strong.

Contents

Acknowledgments

I begin by thanking family and friends for their patience, forbearance, and love of me, even when that poetic fog descended and I disengaged from them in order to go write something down. Thanks to my former teachers and professors, all of whom found promise in my work and encouraged me.

I am indebted to those writers whose invaluable criticism, warmth, support, and words of wisdom proved indispensable. In particular, I'd like to thank Sydney Lea, Robert Morgan, Michael McFee, Richard Tillinghast, Michael Chitwood, Cathy Smith-Bowers, Kathryn Stripling Byer, Andrew Hudgins, Mark Strand, Robert Hass, Alan Shapiro, John Lane, Bret Lott, Mary Jo Salter, Brad Leithauser, John Irwin, and X. J. Kennedy. Special thanks go to Randall Kenan for friendship and talk of music.

I am also grateful to Gallaudet University for its financial support in allowing me to attend such gatherings as the Appalachian Writers' Workshop in Hindman, Kentucky; the Sewanee Writers' Conference in Sewanee, Tennessee; the Bear River Writers' Conference in Walloon Lake, Michigan; the Johns Hopkins University's Conference on Craft in Florence, Italy; and the Palm Beach Poetry Festival in Florida. Wyatt Prunty, Cheri Peters, Keith Taylor, David Everett, and Miles Coon, in kindness, ensured a "room" of my own.

Thanks to my students and to fellow poets around the world, from whom I have learned so much and to whom much is owed. I treasure the time we have spent together. I'm grateful to Bill and Lisa Koelewyn for frequent sanctuary on the island, and to Stephanie Bugen, Dr. Diana Glyer, Jean Calery, Lisa Walters, and Celeste Ploumis, best friends, for seeing me through.

The following poems are dedicated to the late Jim Wayne Miller: *Christmas Dance, Teaching Load, A Colleague's Death, For* the *Living*, and *He Asks Me to Write of Him*. To the memory of John Edward Taylor I bequeath *Telegraph*, *New Linen*, *Upon Learning of Your Death*, *Brigantine Island*, and *Sail*. *In Fog* is for Robert Hass, with gratitude, and *Reprieve* is for Anthony Hecht, may he rest in peace. *A Deaf Man Uses the Telephone* is for Alan Shapiro. *Undone*, *Six-Year Forecast*, and *Waterrock Knob* are for Chuck Baird. To Barry Coopersmith, I dedicate *A Woman's Want*, *Swimming in the Nude*, *Trellis*, *Delray*, and *Rite of Purification*.

Finally, I wish to express my gratitude to the Gallaudet University Press and to Ivey Pittle Wallace, editor extraordinaire, for her unerring advice and inspired guidance in making this book a reality.

Publications

I'd like to express my gratitude to the editors of the following journals in which my poems were previously published:

Appalachian Heritage

For the Living
Teaching Load
Christmas Dance
Some Poems Come
The Children and I Shall
    Meet Again
For Sale

The Asheville Poetry Review

Samaria: Woman at the Well

The Bear River Review

Hats
Guest Room
To Hear Again
Spelling Test

*The Bear River
Writers Respond to War* (Ann
Arbor: Word 'n' Woman Press)

Guest Room

Cellar Roots

Pillars
Only One Life
A Concert
Rites of Purification

College English

Visit

The Comstock Review

Museum of Fine Arts

Crossing Troublesome: Twenty-Five Years of the Appalachian Writers' Workshop (Louisville: Wind Press)	Hindman Poetry Reading
The Journal of Kentucky Studies	Invitation Watching the Weatherman Wheat Wedding Band Tom's Death One Young Wife's Tale Sycamores Michigan Sail Marry Me Lazy Sunday Morning Telegraph Haze Reject Slips
Labyris	Maria
The Missouri Philological Association	Telegraph Sail
Moving Out	Mother
The Ozarks Mountaineer	Ex Libris
Pegasus	Some Poems Come Christmas Dance
The Pine Mountain Sand and Gravel	Snapshots 1–12

Plaza Moons	Bittersweet
	They
	Upon Telling You to Go
	Fall in Love
Soundings	One Young Wife's Tale
	Lazy Sunday Morning
The Southern Review	Mailman
	Home Run
	Mother's Day
SouthLit.com	A Deaf Man Uses the Telephone
storySouth	Flight to India
	India: Step
	Kashmiri Houseboat
	Two Peonies
	Thaw in Karnataka
The Tactile Mind	Julia Sails from Ireland
	Resurrection
	School Store
	The Love Zone ABCs
	Prospectus
	Roxbury Mill
The Threepenny Review	Black and White
Virginia Writing	Uncle Jimmy
Xanadu	Hospital

(xv

Introduction

It all started in the crib. My father, leaning over me with his large frame and wild, wavy, blond hair like Einstein's, pointed to the decoupage lamb on my wooden crib; this lamb was dancing happily in a meadow full of daisies waving in the wind. My father used sign language to show me the word "lamb;" then he fingerspelled "l-a-m-b." I must have imitated him, learning to sign as a baby, for he smiled, signed "Good!" and continued by showing me the daisies, their yellow centers, their green, slender leaves, the act of waving, the wind itself, carefully showing me each letter and how to form it with my fingers.

This continued with my mother. Curled up in her lap, admiring her black hair and dark Irish eyes, I looked to where she pointed in my ABC book. "A" is for apple, "B" is for bear. . . . She would sign and fingerspell each word, then show me the worm in the apple, the bow around the bear's neck, taking my hands into her own and shaping them to the correct letters and signs.

My mother and father were both born hearing, and became deaf through calamity. My mother contracted scarlet fever at about the age of two-and-a-half; my father fell from a tree at eleven years of age and hit his head in just such a way as to cause him to lose his hearing. Both were educated at the elementary and middle school levels in oral methods of communication while secretly signing with their friends and classmates. They were of Irish and Norwegian/Dutch backgrounds, respectively, and had been raised with religious training as well, but back in the 1920s and 1930s, deaf education left a lot to be desired. My mother attended the Detroit Day School for the Deaf run at that time by the Lutheran Church; when she was in high school, her father insisted on a Catholic education, so she attended St. Mary's in Buffalo, New York, and then St. Rita's in Cincinnati, Ohio.

During her junior year, her mother died, necessitating my mother's return to the family. She never graduated from high school, yet held some jobs that she enjoyed, such as working as a seamstress and drape maker at Hudson's department store in Detroit; I remember vividly the drapes in our living room on Burgess Avenue as having an ivory background against which palm trees with ruffled fronds unfurled in an imaginary breeze. While my mother hemmed those drapes, I watched a cartoon show on our new TV, featuring cigar-smoking magpies, Heckle and Jeckle. I remember wondering about the fact that one of them spoke with a Brooklyn accent, the other with a British inflection. How could it be that they didn't sound alike? My mother later worked in the very social world of the Fort Street Post Office in downtown Detroit, visiting old friends there for lunch even long after her retirement.

My father and mother met during a deaf club gathering, began dating, and married shortly thereafter. My father graduated from the Tennessee School for the Deaf in Knoxville, where he had received vocational training in the print shop. He then migrated north, finding a job at the *Detroit Free Press* as a linotype operator in the days before computer-assisted publishing. My poem "Hats" is based on the many different newspaper configurations he would bring home to us at the end of the day. My father loved to go to deaf club events, including bingo nights, picnics and baseball games held on the grounds of the Koepplinger Bakery, and outings on the Detroit River on the boat to Bob-Lo Island. Bob-Lo's amusement park boasted a dance hall called the Pavilion. My parents used to "feel" the beat in the wooden floors and dance all day while we kids happily rode the roller coasters and made cavities sucking on peppermint sticks that were two inches in diameter. Some of these memories show up in my poems.

I am a CODA, a Child of Deaf Adults. I didn't use my voice much before my first day of kindergarten, when I remember signing to my teacher, "My sweater . . . hang where?" The look of horror that crossed over her face and her subsequently hilarious efforts at getting me to speak resulted in five years of speech therapy, where my "auxiliary" teacher rewarded me with a gold star on my forehead every time I could put out the candle by making a proper "p" or "b" sound. I much preferred the world of sign language, the immediate, beautiful, expressive, animated world of fingerspelling and signing all that I wanted to say, all that I needed to ask.

When I was made to talk, I yearned to run home, to hide in the folds of my mother's crepe dress, or on my father's lap, telling him in great detail the shame I felt when another student tattled on me for practicing the words of a spelling bee under my desk, on my hands; if it felt right there, it was how I put it down on my numbered paper. I still, to this day, am tempted to fold my nightgown and place it under my pillow as my parents did during their days in deaf school dormitories. CODAs share similar stories the world over.

We lived in a suburb of Detroit called Walled Lake, near St. William's Catholic Church. My mother's parents, William and Margaret O'Flaherty, had given the land for the church, and had donated the rectory, a log cabin structure that was once the family's summer home. The original church, an imposing stone structure, served as the parish hall, theater, and gym in later years. When I was in the eighth grade, I acted the part of Mary in the school play and sang alto in the choir. Although my parents couldn't hear, they attended every single performance and event. Music was always available in our home, either via variety shows on TV, through the radio and Arthur Godfrey, or on a record player my father had won in a poker game, on which he played Benny Goodman LPs. He wore enormous headphones in an attempt to pick up the rhythm, the bass line, something. He would place his hands on the maple kitchen table, on either side of the phonograph, and lean intently into the vibrations that moved out of the wood.

My mother could speak a few words, words that only we kids could understand. When our friends would visit, each sibling had his or her own way of saying, "Now, my parents are deaf but sometimes they try to talk. It sounds sort of strange. Don't worry: I'll interpret for you." Most of our friends found it charming or at least interesting to be exposed to deaf people. But there were certainly those parents of my friends who didn't want their children playing "over there."

My mother and father encouraged our interest in creative endeavors, including singing and playing musical instruments. When I had graduated (in the fourth grade) from playing the song flute to the clarinet, it was my father who insisted on taking me to a store in Pontiac where he purchased, on time, an Olds. This instrument had such a lovely and mellow tone; it lay in its velvet case like an ancient treasure waiting to be discovered. My father also bought a silver music stand and a metronome. He would faithfully look at the time signature on the sheet music, set the metronome, and then watch me practice, tapping his foot in time to the precise brass arm. My own daughters each played this instrument as they joined high school orchestras and marching bands. It had gathered dust in the attic for many years until they, without prompting, expressed an interest in playing the clarinet their grandfather had purchased so many years before.

My parents made sure there were plenty of novels around the house, and an old set of *Encyclopaedia Britannica* volumes. My dear Aunt Carole supplied me with all manner of books, frilly bathing suits, my first typewriter and steady encouragement. My parents and my aunt were my early critics and fed my brain in earnest.

My first short story was published during the eighth grade, in the school newspaper. It was completely fictitious, about a neighbor boy (I had changed his name, I wrote) who had been bitten by a poisonous snake in our backyard, which ran down to a creek. He manages to make it to the side door of the house, where he rings the bell and then knocks feebly as his life slowly ebbs away. My mother is at home, baking a pie in the kitchen. Because she is deaf, she cannot hear his pleas for help. He dies on the porch; the neighbors blame my mother and have her arrested. The judge realizes the death is not her fault and she is exonerated.

Why did I write such a thing? The faculty, students, and administrators of St. William's School all thought it had been a true story. They believed it was real because of the description, the detail, and my manipulation of scene, language, and image in such a way that the story seemed quite plausible. When my parents read it, they just about died. I think I was trying to evoke sympathy, community understanding, some sort of compassion for the circumstances of many deaf people. Combined in this story was a mild sense of outrage at how frequently the hearing community exhibits prejudicial behavior toward deaf people. I am also ashamed to admit that I benefited, for several months, from the waves of sympathy exhibited by those who thought the snake story was true.

Also in the eighth grade, I wrote my first haiku, in English class. Its content led to a concern that, because I was being raised by deaf parents, I was inordinately depressed. I was forced to go into counseling, with a school psychologist who watered his artificial plants. Here's the poem:

VIETNAM

Planes zoom overhead
and all in Danang lie dead.
The silent bomb falls.

My observations of those whose good intentions nonetheless further false and stereotypical thinking about the abilities of deaf people sometimes also appear as themes in my work. I wrote a scathing poem about this psychologist. It is still on the wall in my office and cannot be repeated here. Sometimes CODAs are treated by behavioral, medical, and school personnel as if we are science experiments just waiting to burst into flames.

Then there was the time my mother was in Hudson's, at the candy counter, trying to buy some assorted chocolates for a Christmas box to send to some relatives. The salesperson immediately assumed that my mother was mentally challenged, and simply turned away, refusing to engage her in any fashion, disappearing though the curtained doorway that led to the back room. Or the time when a drugstore clerk called the police after thinking that my mother had stolen an item that had simply fallen into her shopping basket and that she had not set on the cashier's counter to pay for. This sense of outrage still informs some of my poetry. Watching some of the discrimination my parents endured and feeling their frustration are forces that occasionally find their voice in my work. My mother once told me that when her parents had company, she would be put in a closet, released only after the last guest had departed. Some of those experiences have made their way into my poems, as have some of my memories of life in our own family, like the Christmas parties at the deaf club.

And then there is a great deal of experience, expressed in some of my poetry, as my parents' interpreter. I was making phone calls to doctors' offices and other agencies as early as age four. If I missed an important call in the middle of the night while sleeping, I was usually punished. Nonetheless, my overall feeling is one of gratitude for and celebration of being a quasi-member of two cultures, even as that identity was often one of confusing and overlapping allegiances. Some of this identity conflict also appears in my life and, therefore, my work. I am actually a little more comfortable in the deaf community than in the hearing world, and yet I love music, and I love sounds like the scraping of figure skates on ice or the grinding noise made by truckers as they are downshifting. I love to say favorite words out loud, slowly, like "amalgamated" or "Palomino." Even when my hearing siblings and I get together, we often use sign language rather than speech. I attach sounds to motion, as when wheat stalks are rustled by the breeze. When I speak, I often stumble over words and their pronunciations, preferring to make myself understood by signing.

When I am in a signed conversation, or when watching an ASL poet, or when teaching my students at Gallaudet University, I feel whole, uniquely at home, complete. When I am attending a presentation at which there is an interpreter, I will invariably watch the interpreter. I often volunteer as an interpreter in the deaf community or in the local schools, as a way of remaining connected to my parents, who are no longer alive. When I was teaching at hearing universities, prior to becoming a faculty member at Gallaudet, my "deaf side" felt lonely. This desire to stay involved, to be a part of the deaf community, is a need I cannot forsake. I think this need is also what drives the more visual aspects of my work. Now and then, I have included snippets of signed, ASL conversations in my poems as well.

Describing the shimmer of a calm, glassy lake in the moonlight; the white, fluffy petals of a peony; the way icicles drip— all derive from my visual childhood. The imagist nature of my poems finds a basis in looking, in using my eyes for information about the world, about my loved ones, about myself. This ardent and constant looking shows up in my work, in the visual images I use to contain the emotion behind the poem. The acts of seeing and of illustrating are at the root of my poetry, the words serving as concrete depictions of observation and experience.

I believe that not speaking much, relying instead on sign language and visual cues from the world around me, has given me an advantage. There is entirely too much clatter in the world, and silence is a kind of balm. Yet there remains that human need to connect, to share one's life, and so I began to write, partly out of boredom, partly out of loving the reactions I got from my second-grade friends, partly, in the eighth grade, out of seeing my name in print in the school newspaper.

Now, I realize, I write to stave off isolation, to reach out for another. When you are the child of deaf parents, it sometimes happens that when you cry, no one comes, at least not immediately. You learn a kind of self-reliance that often makes it difficult to trust another person, something that relationships of a romantic nature later in life teach you about, with varying results. In these pages of poetry, there is a range of emotion expressed; it has been my purpose to describe feelings we all share in ways that are decidedly visual.

One critic has written that my poems are "painterly." Perhaps it is no coincidence that my favorite artists are the French impressionists and that my favorite poets are the imagists. I dislike enormously poems that are overly abstract, cerebral, or explanatory, or that make vague allusions to things only those living in rarefied academic circles could relate to. My personal snobbery aside, I respond most vigorously to those poems that bring me to a place I can envision or to memorable characters, events, or even to a thimble-sized element that makes me see the entirety of the poet's point, the way someone once described loneliness as being akin to a spiderweb under lawn furniture in the rain, dripping.

Ezra Pound had this to say about one of his briefest poems, written about an experience he had in Paris:

In a Station of the Metro

> The apparition of these faces in the crowd;
> Petals on a wet, black bough.

Three years ago in Paris I got out of a "metro" train at La Concorde, and saw suddenly a beautiful face, and then another and another, and then a beautiful child's face, and then another beautiful woman, and I tried all that day to find words for

what this had meant to me, and I could not find any words that
seemed to me worthy, or as lovely as that sudden emotion. . . .

I realized quite vividly that if I were a painter, or if I had,
often, that kind of emotion, or even if I had the energy to get
paints and brushes and keep at it, I might found a new school
of painting, of "non-representative" painting, a painting that
would speak only by arrangements in colour. . . . That is to say,
my experience in Paris should have gone into paint . . .

(See a republication of this essay in Pound's *Gaudier-Brzeska: A Memoir*
[1916; London: New Directions, 1960], 86–89.)

Pound's idea certainly gave rise to a number of image-driven
works, and many poets, modern and contemporary, are indebted
to him. I have found the imagist idea particularly inspiring.
Somehow, when I see a Michigan birch tree, with its whiteness
and its curling bark, I am reminded of the loss of innocence, of (xxv
how we cannot return to the times of our youth, and of how
specific memories are tied to the particular landscapes in which
they occurred. If I am writing a poem about my son's broken leg,
I find it wasteful to write about my maternal horror, my sense of
panic, of moving in that impossible slow-motion to reach him,
to call for help; I find it much more true and effective to describe
the bone, shattered and protruding from the skin, the jagged
shards stretching marbled tissue and sinew. The reactions of my
readers are all the proof I need that my words conveyed exactly
what I saw; as a result, the emotion is much more powerfully
shared than if I had frittered away the intensity of the observa-
tion with abstraction.

Hence, it is a seeing, and seeing again, that shapes my work. It
is the direct result of being raised by deaf parents, whose entire
method of communicating with me was primarily through our
hands and eyes, through a touch on the shoulder. Concrete.
Tactile. Animated. Expressive.

Many of the poems in this collection have been published before. Many of them are not directly about the CODA experience; some are. Nonetheless, they are all deeply influenced by a desire to create a visual set of images that convey the meaning, the substance, the "meat" of the poem's intention. Several of the poems are about my parents, their lives, what they endured, the discrimination they faced. Most celebrate and express gratitude for a life lived in spite of sadness or loss. All are an effort to reach a reader who can share in this decidedly human business of getting up daily to embrace the unexpected. I am grateful and honored that others might enjoy reading my poetry; I often refer to writing as a sacred enterprise, as an obsession, as an act of facing the unavoidable, as a kind of sweet agony. The incorporation of the visual, which emanates from my experiences as a CODA, is an element essential to my ability to write at all.

Most of this work is autobiographical in nature. Some poems rely on the flexibility of poetic license. A few poems are wholly imagined; nonetheless, the germane point is couched in the cross threads of the woven tale, the "made thing," the *poeien*. And while the vast majority of these offerings seems to be about loss and woe, I wish to assure the reader that I have lived a full and largely happy life, a persistent optimism being one of my lucky faults.

One critic has written that my poems ". . . set you up and then knock you out." I'm not so sure about the impact of the work but it is an accurate observation of my method, which is to rely on the visual and to allow the abstract to find its way through the tangible. Like the imagist poets, I prefer to let the actual, the specific, do the "work" of revealing that which is more ephemeral, more peripheral, less concrete. Even in the poems that are not directly about being the child of deaf adults, or that do not have as their subject any aspect of working, living, or breathing within the deaf community, that influence and exposure form the foundation of my approach. This is why I am drawn to art, to mobiles, to the fluttering of leaves in the wind. This is why my eyes immediately dart to anything nearby that is moving. If someone near me raises his hand, I'm on alert, waiting for the ensuing message, even if he's just hailing a cab.

This is a unique and mysterious life. It is with a sense of joy and gratitude that I regard my parents' lives, all that they endured, their contributions to my well-being, and their encouragement.

Moon on the Meadow

Asylum

I paint my walls
a harvest wheat,
Van Gogh's straw hat,
his maize reeds fraying.

Against this hue,
blue hydrangeas
crowd the stone
cream pitcher.

I would drink this milk,
this gold light:
periwinkle,
powder slate.

Some Poems Come

Some poems come like rain:
    torrential
    gales of rushing wind
    brush fire, wild.
Some poems come like creeks in spring:
    thrashing water
    birdsong
    gurgling loam.
Some seem firm, cool:
    urgent fossils pressed into rock
    fragment thoughts
    ferns.

Then there is the dust:
    a time to wait
    a seeing spell.

I sit on the bank, still:
    the quiet smell of leaves
    bedrock
    mold.

Julia Sails From Ireland

My mother tossed a coin into my hands.
My father knelt in the sheep shed, clutching the
knotted beams.   Julia Garland Murphy 1861

We started from Clondalkin, bucked
all night in the splintered yellow wagon.
Plumes of silver steam huffed
from the horses' flaring nostrils.
We wheeled away, alone
along the rutted road to Sligo.

Married three shy days beforehand
in the chapel at St. Margaret's,
we booked passage to Detroit
and we waited for the tide.
His hands in deep wool pockets,
Jamie fingered his gold band.

He looked at me and wavered;
gangplanks jutted from the pier.
How we waved good-bye to strangers,
waved good-bye to boats in dry dock.
We wrapped ourselves in newsprint,
slept on barrels, turning westward.

The choppy waves' white minch
slapped hard against the prow,
blew upon the deck's wide platform,
drained in sheets like mam's wash water.

We could see the spray through portholes
as we counted out the days.

As we crossed the roiling ocean,
Jamie spoke of farms and berries,
of a homestead, unborn children,
but he could not meet my gaze.
With his foot upon the rail,
he stroked my hair, crooned hoarsely:

There now, Julie, hush.
It's all right. Don't you cry.

Mailman

After she scoured the shirtwaists and linens,
after the bluing was poured out on rocks,
my grandmother hung the laundry on lines
stretched between two towering maples,
their dust-silted leaves upturning in air.
She was young then, supple, bending to basket
like willow to pond. Loose tendrils escaped
her upswept hair: auburn, unruly, luxurious.
Horse hooves clopped, scudding the earth.
She turned to see William, the county mailman,
wearing the boots he'd saved ten months to buy.
A faint blush appeared; she wiped her hands
and smoothed her apron, walking to the narrow lane.
From a satchel he drew a packet of letters, bound
with string, from cousins in Kildare and Cork.
He wished her good day and bowed from the waist,
a lock of black hair falling to his eyes. She could not
speak, not even when he clucked his tongue and set
the roan to trotting. But he'd be back tomorrow.

5

Black and White

In one shot my mother wears a strapless gown.
Her raven hair waves down to her shoulders;
a diamond clip sweeps a stubborn strand.
The heart-shaped bodice, smooth folds
of black satin, narrows to the waistline,
reels away to layers of silky silver print.

Her legs are crossed. One dangling shoe
peeks out at twelve men standing at the bar.
They nurse bottles of beer, angled
heads tipped in her direction. In
shiny shark suits and neck knots, loosening,
they drink her in, oblivious to the cameraman

who will become my father.
Through the aperture, his lenses focus:
his shuttered heart opens and gasps.
Later, in the darkroom, he will ease the solution
as her eyes swim toward him. He will enlarge
many copies; he will hang her up to dry.

Snapshots 1–12

The lamb on my crib dances in a meadow.
My ABC book. Ceramic fish on the bathtub wall.

In a ruffled bathing suit, I plop down.
A plastic blow-up pool. Colored rings.

Next, my clown and toy piano.
A red rocking chair. Hardwood floors.

Twelve cousins line up to jump off the hassock.
Again and again. Uncle Bill sleeps on the couch.

Mama's hand slips from mine. Green lake
Water enshrouds me. My lungs burn for air.

I stand on a barstool in a pink pouffy dress.
Mama doesn't know. Daddy holds me steady.

Here lies the daughter who slept through the call
That granny made when granddad died.

Brother and I are smiling. Later, he will
Bloody my eye with a baseball bat.

Now I wear a First Communion veil.
White prayer book. Rosary beads lightly held.

Our snow fortress. Ramparts. Terry Rogers
Throws ice balls. He may like me.

Perched in the window, I sing hymns in Latin.
The world asleep, the stars my true confessors.

Dad rubs balloons on his chest. They cling
To the wall. Dad drives away.

Steps

I ponder the childhood
spent walking strange woods.
I found an old fire pit once,
a circle of logs pushed together.
Seating for whom? Dusty hobos?
A discarded car, rusted,
the mohair seats wormy,
striped with the grease
of an unknown life,
its fortune played out.
A deer's head, cast in stone,
the creekbed, dry,
tall weeds grazing the fog.

When winter iced the pond,
I skated to Ben's farm,
walked the horses, their breath
plumes of indignation. We left
warm stalls for crusty land,
steps uneven, insistent stomping,
straining against the bit
for the known path back.

I walked on past time to be in,
my parents alive with worry,
my frozen feet no longer connected,
my need to name the night air
impossible.

Brushing My Mother's Hair

At the age of five I hunkered down
behind my mom's best Queen Anne chair
to study the cover of *Life* magazine.
Sophia Loren sat at a diner counter
coolly contemplating a cup of tea
while Elvis Presley, sitting to her left,
examined her cleavage.
The expression on his face wandered
from hushed awe to wolfish hunger.
I looked down at my then-meager chest,
despaired of love, and turned the page.

Before dinner, I watered red geraniums
thriving in basement windows;
from under the Christmas tree,
I gathered dead pine needles
in hand-carved wooden bowls, stirring
carefully, for my make-believe husband
would be home any minute, wanting
his supper and a bright, happy kitchen.
He would come sweeping in, kiss me
on the cheek, lay his newspaper on the table,
sniff the air and sign, "Dinner what? Smell good."

At bedtime, I watched my mother
at her vanity, removing makeup.
A silver-plated brush in hand, she began
methodical strokes, smoothing out the tangles,
curling the ends under, turning her head
this way and that, her arms graceful in the air.

I asked for a turn, the brush heavy in my hand.
As I styled my mother's hair, I added clips
and pins, her best diamond comb, spit curls
to an upswept do that rivaled any model's.
I thought it all so beautiful.

Cunningham's Drug Store

Up and down the aisles my deaf mother walked,
a red basket on her arm, picking up and putting down
this or that first-aid product, this or that shoelace pair.

This went on for hours while I stood on one foot
and then the other, shifting my weight,
watching other shoppers choose, pay, and go.

I gravitated to the toy section, to the plastic pink
high-heeled slippers, a glittering daisy at the toes,
while my mother sniffed a bottle of Evening in Paris.

We stopped at the lunch counter, ordered cream puffs
from Sanders' and Cokes; she gave me a quarter for the
juke box and I dreamily listened to Elvis croon.

She watched my face, pretended to dance along,
waving her arms, snapping her fingers. I sank
below the stool; the manager told her to leave.

Hats

Every evening we kids would gather
on the front porch steps, an assembled,
motley menagerie of stripes and polka dots,
shorts and T-shirts, torn denim,
hugging our scabby knees, waiting
for the '57 baby blue Buick to pull
into the driveway. We'd run to the door,
pulling at the handle like mad while our
tired, deaf father leaned against collective weight
to barrel his way through the horde of grubby
fingers, smeared faces, our insistence that he
hand over that day's goods: newspaper hats.

Designed and folded during midday breaks as
the linotypes hummed and clattered away,
the hats held the daily comics, the editorial page,
headlines from distant lands, ads from Hudson's,
where our deaf mother sewed drapes for the rich.

No two hats were ever the same.

Mine was like Napoleon's, with wings enough
to lift me straight to my father's shoulders.
My brothers got Navy sailors' hats, or those like Robin Hood's,
or a Greek boat captain's, or the tam of Robbie Burns,
or like an officer from the French Foreign Legion.

Off we'd run to new adventures, wild conquests,
while our father sagged in the easy chair,
watching the news without sound.

Deaf Club Christmas Bazaar

Long tables, decked in holiday holly,
staffed by the eager, line the dining room
at the deaf club. Hand-crafted items for sale
abound, everything from dolls to quilts to
white elephant knickknacks and piggy banks.

Metal folding chairs huddle near the bar
where the deaf people sit, playing gin rummy;
only the sound of cards slapping,
of chair legs scraping the floor, can be heard
as the action heats up.

The Santa waves all the girls onto his lap.
His boozy breath, laced with cigarettes,
sears the back of my neck. He bounces
me on his knee, then signs the question:
Christmas time. You want what? Santa bring.

I want that fireplace fan on the corner table
that my father says is too expensive. It's a cinnamon
and peach floral design and the bracket is brass.

My mother signs, *Do? Do? For? For?*
No fireplace home. Money waste. Why?

I know I will die without this fan.
I start to cry. Father John asks, "What's the matter?"

My mother signs, *My daughter. Finish crazy.*

That nice man, Nick, who always jokes around,
comes over. He takes my hand, as if he is going to
kiss it, like Maurice Chevalier in *Gigi*.
Last minute, he kisses his own hand; this makes me laugh.
I stop crying. He has no wife, no kids.
He signs, *Fan. How much cost? I buy.*
Why baby make sad? For? For?

He walks me to the fan table. My mother rolls her eyes.

A Deaf Man Uses the Telephone

The dashboard lights frame
my parents' faces. For once their
hands lie still, all signing silent.
My father's bear paws bristle blond
fur, guide the Studebaker's wheel.
Mother's long fingers curl
the clasp of a sleek, satin purse.

We drive from the lakes toward
the city and its stoplights. We
scritch, bump, and smooth
from gravel to highway, the tires
loving asphalt as they do.
I lie on the back seat, grow small
as raindrops on rear windows.

Telephone poles, regular as metronomes,
line our route, their slick, black
ropes slung like licorice, like vines
from tree to jungle tree. I think
they relay secret code words,
buzzing, fraying in copper collusion.
My dad gets their message,

knowing where to go.

Home Run

In a pert scarf over pincurls and waves,
my mother, in seersucker capris,
set tables for the deaf club picnic
on the grounds of Koepplinger's Bakery.
Back behind the loading dock, ladies
snapped red and white checkered vinyl
as if making beds for food, for catsup
and mustard, relish in squeezable bottles.
Our fathers played baseball, huffing along.
They skinned their knees, pulled muscles,
bellied up to barbecues and coolers,
grilled hotdogs and chicken breasts,
swilling beer, leering at the teenaged girls
they hoped were watching (they weren't).

We settled in for potato salad. The kids fought
over deviled eggs, threw water balloons,
chomped on wads of bubble gum.
Babies slept in strollers, the sun turning
their hairs even whiter in its glare,
its rays bouncing off the scoreboard,
where "Koepps" and "Visitors" finally faded
as evening fell, mosquitoes swarming.
My parents lingered under one last light.
Sad to say goodnight, they signed and signed
to anyone still standing. The parking lot opened
its gravel to the stars. I picked up a pebble,
slid it down in my pocket, climbed onto
our backseat and stretched out for home.

The Deaf Club Sails to Bob-Lo Island

On the Fort Street dock of the Detroit River,
we waited to see her smokestack huff.
The bell clanged twice as the pipe organ
tune sang out over poop deck bunting.
Clutching grimy tickets, wearing name
tags, sucking on peppermint logs,
we stood in line, the gangplank's tilt
just enough to stretch our calves.
I shoved right past my baby brothers,
first to board, to pet the captain's parrot.

Our parents bought us snow cones,
settled onto benches, signed to us,
Hold on to the rails. I perched atop
the picnic basket, my crow's nest
over tree-lined waters, gray and languid.
I yelled, "Ahoy!" when I spied the flags.
Wooden coasters rattled, their shrieking
patrons hurtling near the crowded midway.
We scrambled to attention. The first mate
threw the ropes, pulled to, dismissed his crew.

We rode the rides till we were hot and nauseated.
Shade pulled us to the vast pavilion where
parents two-stepped, cheek to cheek,
or swiveled hips like Elvis Presley.
Mother's dress swirled yellow, full.

When Daddy spun and dipped her low,
she came up laughing. How did they know
to move their feet, which steps to take?
How did they feel the drum line's beat?
I saw them dance to private music.

School Store

Down the glossy halls of St. William School,
smelling of Pine Sol and starched nuns' clothing,
lay the Tuesday morning treasure-trove: the school store.
Pencils, fat pink erasers, scissors that wouldn't cut butter,
stacked up tall under the glass counter.

All I wanted was paper. Blue Horse Tablets.
Loose leaf. Lined. Reams of it.
There weren't enough sheets for the words I had.

Sister Lucy Michael, moustache and all,
made us fill theme books with the
Fruits of the Holy Spirit,
the Seven Deadly Sins.
I never could tell the difference.

I wanted to twist those Seven Deadly Sins over,
lick their underbellies.
Gluttony and sloth sounded pretty good when it came to
Bobby Triplett with those violet eyes,
his Fabian-style black forelock swirl.

He bought me some of that thirty-cent paper and
passed me a note. It read,
"Sister Mary Peters waters her artificial plants.
Meet me behind the bleachers tonight."

Mama wouldn't let me out past supper,
so I breathed frost against the window,
traced his name in the icy parchment.

Spelling Test

Under the knife-gnawed desk,
my hands knuckled past
clumps of gum, rested in my lap,
waited for the first word,
the bee to begin. *Amalgamated.*

Mrs. Skevold paced the classroom.
With red lips pursed, she succinctly
enunciated each syllable, repeating
our weekly words, her elocution
grand in my hungry ears.

Amalgamated. My finger tried
a few faltering letters, backed
up, tried again, fumbled.
I erased the mistakes with a wave,
then found the path: *a-m-a-l* . . .

When it felt right on my hands,
when I had worked it through,
I raised my pencil to the page,
the numbered lines
falling into place.

To Hear Again

How can I enter their world of deafness?

When I was twelve, my parents built
a round, above-ground pool
with bottom folds of excess vinyl
wide enough to anchor there.
I dove down deep to grasp the blue
and slippery liner. I held on,
letting water seep into my ears.
Even after exhaled bubbles lifted
to the rippling surface, I stayed below,
the stillness pressing against my skin,
against my sense of the outer world,
its rattling chatter, its constant
noise.

My lungs began to burn. I lost
the urge to gulp, grew calm as
sunlight streamed above me.
My hair grew long in mermaid waving
while my feet floated high aloft,
small and foreign, pale as clouds.
I closed my eyes, abandoned thought,
listened to silence. I tried to feel
the permanence of nothing.
When I could bear no more, I swam;
rustling branches framed my rising
as birdsong pierced the air,
riotous.

Mother

In my childhood attic,
third-floor haven,
my mother comes to tell me
the phone has been ringing.
Her bare feet feel vibrations
on the sun-warmed floors.

While Christmas shopping,
my mother holds
a porcelain music box
to her ears. She dances
to the far-off tune,
her dark eyes gleaming.

At a wedding, a flautist's
languid notes lilt on the air.
My mother, who cannot hear,
leans forward, attentive
to the dip and sway of his body.
She signs to me:

It sounds like butterflies.

Roof

In the August heat, my father hands me a hammer,
roofing nails, a sheet of tar paper, thirty-pound.

We roll it over plywood, hide the knots and cracks,
tack down the vast expanse. We unbind stacks of shingles,

rough in their diamond-crusted surface, sticky in the sun.
We line them up in terraced patterns, our feet steady

on anchored blocks. We lift the vent frames, tent
the ridgeline, start down the other side. We do not talk.

Losing Faith

It is my father's funeral.
We are huddled at the Mass,
kneeling, going through the motions
at all the right moments.

I interpret for my mother:
Who is that rabbi? Those relatives?
Why are the roses white, not red?
I have no explanations.

My hands move swiftly from Kyrie
to Agnus Dei. I hope the signs are clear
and somewhat sweet in this time
of solemn grief. My mother nods,

smiles, sways to hymns she cannot
hear. A toddler falls and bangs her head;
two teenagers snicker. The priest glares
at them with his one good eye.

Inside my father's casket,
his body washed and oiled,
a pale wool tallis enfolds him,
its fringes lying still.

We line up at the holy rail.
The Host sticks to my tongue;
the wine bites like vinegar.
There's only so much I can swallow.

The casket wheels away.
Men in gray suits, soft shoes,
load my father into the hearse,
his stone mezuzah in my hand.

Visit

My mother, who does not hear,
visits and is bored.
"It's so quiet here."
She wanders from room to room,
fingering the curtains,
looking out the windows at nothing,
she says, but "all that land."
Old hickories rise, dropping nuts
on brushy weeds and honeysuckle vines.
Late raspberries barely ripen;
the dog slumps in the flower beds.

We sit down together,   (27
the round oak table
a ring of reconciliation.
We use our hands to talk,
our words visible in the air,
our faces too animated.

Our lives have been lived
through symbols passed between us
like tea in flowered cups,
slowly stirred,
honey and lemon.

Resurrection

The fog's dim chill enshrouds
my dying mother.
She wisps upon its icy needles.
Her voice is found the next
morning wrapped in gauze.
Translucent as sea glass,
she speaks aloud in my dream.
Her hummingbird words
lick nectar from my ears,
vanish into thin rain.

School for the Deaf

As a child, I held my mother's
hand as the scrolled iron doors
clanged shut in the sagging elevator.
It creaked to the home economics
floor, where the girls all learned
to mend and make, to cook, to keep
ordered, happy homes. She had come
for her class reunion, a gathering
of graduates who by then understood
that the nuns, in their starched wimples,
had taught them nothing useful at all.

Her well-intentioned parents had sent
her away for a Catholic education,
its influence meant to ward off evil,
to keep her safe in the bosom of the Church.
The children signed secretly, their knuckles
raw and scabbed; the Sisters of Charity
wielded wooden rulers with a steely edge.

Fifty years later, I return to the classrooms.
Back in the home ec hallway, I stop before
a group photo I have come six hundred miles to see.
In 1925, my mother, a sturdy girl,
wears a white, long-sleeved shift,
the dropped waist lined with lace,
a low bow at the back. Her dark hair
is cut with straight-across bangs,
the rest chin-length, curled under.
Her expression is somber. She is tanned.

I remember stories about the times
she ran away, lying on a hillside in the sun,
blackberry juice staining the bodice
no amount of washing could clean.

Deaf Like Me

After the first class, a student approaches.
He is excited, enthused, eager to sign to me
his thoughts and hopes for the term.
He goes on and on about how well I sign,
how much he hates hearing teachers,
how communication is everything.
He thinks I am Deaf. He is out
the door before I can stop him.

Later, in the cafeteria, he shares
our conversation with his friends.
He bemoans the inept and awkward
signing of those he can't understand.
Again and again he lets them know
how much he despises the hearing faculty.
"I told her, too!" he proudly signs.
Their mouths fall open.

He won't believe them when they tell him.
"But she signs like us," he tries to exclaim.
"I get everything she says. No confusion!"
Fearing an offense, he sends an apology.
The e-mail reads, "I am sooooooooooo
sorry. I thought you were Deaf, like me."
I smile and type, "No problem.
See you in class. Thanks."

Mother's Day

After the sheep were lathered,
rinsed, and the great sluice opened,
we walked across the pebbled basin,
our rubbers mucking in the silt.

In the brisk air, a mist gathered
in the valley below, the chill
soon edging beneath our skin,
driving us in for warmth.

The ladies rose from a fireside circle,
made room, brought tea, biscuits,
and clabbered cream. They talked
of shearing, carding, spinning.

Needles clacked in gnarled hands.
Strands of yarn in heather tones,
grays and greens, soft lavender, blue,
lay at their feet in baskets of balls.

A flicker in their fingers' movement,
a lightness in their rhythm and grace,
took me back to my mother's lessons;
my hands in hers, I learned the turns:

that same way of casting on, perfect
loops adjoining the next. Linear wool
became a sweater, bloomed into hats
and mittens, scarves against the cold.

Miller Avenue

Across the cotton twine strung
between our bedroom windows,
we sang the Indian maiden
password song, our signal to meet:
Hi lo, eenie meenie caca
um cha cha, pee wa wa.
We dropped the cans to rattle against
clapboard siding, ran to the hemlock
and the oak stump where we hatched
our plans to ride the horse D'Artagnan,
to puzzle over boys, their habits and emissions.
We played with Barbie, her breasts exposed
in Ken's convertible, the nipples painted on
in silver nail polish. Her little sister,
Skipper, lay on the back seat in matching
shorts and twinset, her plastic heels,
innocent, immune, uninterested.

November, 1963

The first time I saw my mother
cry, her tears fell to a blue bowl,
splayed and pooled on cookie dough,
the dark chips jagged and shiny.
No salt needed now, she signed,
her gaze fixed on the flickering screen,
the TV perched on a shelf near the sink.

In the kitchen that morning, silence
cooled linoleum floors, my bare feet
pricked with goose bumps, achy.
Mother sagged on the chrome stool,
arms crossed above her belly.

Later, I watched as his wife turned to climb
the back seat, a purse on her arm,
her perfect pillbox hat, to gather his head
to her cheek, to reach for something
already gone, her eyes frantic, her eyes
already bright with grief. My mother's eyes,
too, gone from me, our shopping, our baking
set aside for the day, the blue bowl
beading up when the fire went out.

Uncle Jimmy

In the roaring swell of darkness
    he lay there, gasping.
So I left the valleys of Virginia,
    crossed the paths of glaciers and mill towns,
    to Michigan,
    till I reached his bed,
    his side,
    his memory.
Damp nurses in sterile gowns
    bathed him, murmuring.
Perfect tubes pumped oxygen,
    glucose, morphine.
His gaunt legs twitched;
his soft skin gleamed.
Gray hair, wild and matted,
    crowned the brooding brow.
We were all there,
    averting our eyes.

After the hospital,
I drove around the frozen lake.
Men cracked the yielding ice for fish.
Kids in bright mittens skated out too far,
    testing their weight.
        Where is the limit line?
I was young here, once:
    the cry of loon,
        the arc of northern lights.
All songs, all dreams
    collapse:

His face,
the hollow socket.

So we brought him home
to die under the dim light
in my grandparents' dining room,
their wedding cake hardened
in the china cabinet.

The mortician's men washed and dressed him,
placed his body on the rolling pallet,
lumbered down the floral staircase,
past his sister, who clutched at me.
They wheeled him out to the shiny black Caddy,
laid him in the rear among the blanching lilies.

Later, we filed past the walnut casket,
past the aunts who had not spoken in years,
past as they hugged one another,
their bosoms heaving in doubled grief.
We followed the hearse
while neighbors flew the Irish flag
and wept.

Missa Liturgis

Introit

After communion in the stained-glass chapel,
the priest forewarned our Latin class. "Ladies,"
he intoned, "men can smell your monthly blood."
Sister Ignatius fainted and fell to the floor.
Girls began to cry; one ran to call her mother.

Absolution

He reeked of cigars and bay rum cologne.
His long, black Caddy lay parked at the track
or the poker game, his stations of the cross.
But he cried at babies' baptisms, cradled
their heads, wept for his own lapsed contrition.

Consecration

In a hotel room in Chicago, one young virgin
strips away her catechism. Lying nude before
him, she reaches for the Tree of Knowledge.
She hums, "In Him Is My Salvation," offers
the sacrificial cup. He shouts, "Alleluia!"

Benediction

Each time she nears the sacred altar,
he slips the host, his finger on her tongue.
His secret wink confirms their communion;
his hands coax the final blessing: "The Body
of Christ," he moans. "Amen," she cries.

Samaria: Woman at the Well

I.

My earthenware jugs are cracked.
The well's run dry and dust bites my tongue.
Thirsty? There is no chance for water.
But then Jesus drives up in his SUV,
wearing Birkenstocks and a five-day beard.
His hands are lined and brown.
Curls of wood shavings fall from his shoulders.
Jesus glances into the well, spits softly.
"What the hell," he says. "Dry as a bone."
I nod, then scan the sky for miracles.
Jesus shuffles his feet, reties his bandana,
hitches his overalls and looks me over.
"What's your name?" he asks.

II.

Jesus loves poetry and babies,
BBQ, corn on the cob, and a cold beer.
He is a can-do man on a mission.
Jesus talks philosophy, sings
like James Taylor, repairs small
engines. He eats whatever I cook,
stays mostly sober.
Jesus whittled a dowsing rod, walked
the land in a checkerboard pattern
holding out for water, waiting on a storm.

III.
Jesus died when lightning hit the shed.
He'd been welding a seam, the torch bright
with blue heat. We buried him
on the hillside, like he wanted.
When the creek began to rise, the mudslide
carried his coffin clear to town.
Fish multiply in the pond now.
Water fills the well, but it seeps
through my pottery
as I climb the hill home.

Invitation

Your skepticism
is gray and jaded.
Jilted three times
by the lady at the gate,
you close your door,
lock it tight,
withdraw to cavernous
stone rooms of dusk,
retire to the fire,
the only heat you'll face.

Tulips leap at your steps,
thrust oranges and melon reds.
Forsythias bloom yellow,
heads heavy on the stalk.
Willows tear lemon-green leaves
while the air trembles. Loons
call in the pool of night.

You don't see them.
You don't hear them.
Blind and deaf, you turn
away from me.
I would invite you,
entice you.
Embrace it all
though thorns of fear
claw at you.

Do not cover your eyes: I am beautiful.
Open your ears: I speak of love.

Eagle's Nest

The last I knew about him
fields of barley, curly hair
yellow glint in dark eyes flashing
was enough to satisfy.

But a scattered lifetime later
I flew back down to the mountains,
bought a flashlight, a box of matches,
tins of crabmeat, a case of Merlot.

I waved to his shy brother,
holed up in my high cabin,
strung out and hung up
on the jagged limestone peaks.

I dozed awhile, then startled
to the jangling telephone:
his voice rasped, whiskey-laden,
too familiar, wanted, lean.

I heard the cuss and growl
of his yearning, cradled crooning,
his urgent whisper needling,
low, insistent, wired, soothing.

The phone burned through my fingers
August sun on our bare skin
his length a long, brown shadow
on the grassy, dappled bald

A braided wreath of longing
    rose and crowned our golden heads
    our loving steady, frenzied
    in the wind across the crag.

There was no peace then, ever—
just an echo to his call:
    Are you still there? Remember?
It's important. This is me.

Undone

The artist plays the tape she sent last winter,
paces to fiddles and Celtic pipes, avoids,
comes near, the vast and holy canvas. Wielding
dull knives, he scratches an edge of blue,
a flame-white line, a ridge of smooth plateaus,
the urge to fill each inch, every hollow plane.

He tries all night to forget her, yet a slice
of thigh, a curve, winged blades appear, possess
his tortured, fine abstraction. His frenzy
mounts and spills itself. The artist
steps aside, wipes his hands, pretends
he doesn't see her yellow scarf

(43

hanging, tied to the door's bright latch.

Six-Year Forecast

In your studio, I ask all about you,
your childhood, your sorrows, each iota
of your becoming the man I love. I watch
you paint: acrylic tubes lined up by shade.

In the brewery, your arm on my chair,
my shoulder nestled into yours, you eat from
my plate, taste my dish in front of friends, help
yourself to what is mine, as though we both belong.

You walk your bike; I drive to the corner.
When we meet at the junction, two crows mate.
As the black birds tangle, we look into each
other's eyes. I turn down the slippery slope.

At the truck rental, before you move away,
your lips slightly suction mine as we sigh
the fond farewell. As you drive off, salmon
clouds swim and cross the purpling skies.

After the play, we sleep near ocean waves.
You pat the bed. We lie again in simple bliss.
The candles burn to puddled discs,
their black wicks crisp and crumbling.

Now we scheme to meet again,
the distance notwithstanding.
I fly to you, my baggage stowed;
you're running toward the tarmac.

Hospital

I have come to find you in a panic,
through strangled traffic, too many cops;
when I finally get there, more bodies
line the hallway. Your students,
it seems, cannot get enough of you,
either; they stand and shift their
weight, chatter and laugh, yearn for a break
in the fear-filled nightmare that is their
adolescence while gnawed by the thought of you
downed and in a hospital gown.

I elbow my way through letter jackets,
gang insignia, to the barricade of bulldog nurses
who sniff with superiority, who must ascertain
my relation to the patient. He is theirs, after all.
What could be more intimate, what better claim
upon him than wiping his body, drawing his blood,
inserting the bladder tube? They think they know
his history, his treatment, our prognosis.
To them I'm a distraction, a woman in a shawl,
distraught, bacterium, a rival.

But then, from the railed bed, you rise to call my name.

Mercenary

Here now gleams the silver point,
its galvanized shaft blue in shadow,
hilt and hasp, my sharp conclusion:
sword of your indifference, honed.

Shall I lunge? Be pierced? Parry now
or flee? I wear no mask, no vest
of mesh. I wield no glancing saber.

You pin me in love's grasp, slice tissue,
vein. Blood glistens on the blade.

Your heart, protected, rusts in armor.

Truncated

Here is what she meant to say:

I don't know where
my blood ends and yours begins,
where my skin is not grafted to yours,
where my heart beat has no echo.
Like vines intermingled,
root, leaf, flower,
all veined and pulsing,
we cranny into rock ledge,
stretch toward light,
yet rest, together,
quiet in shadow.

He settled into a separate bed,
drew the quilt up,
turned away.

Here is what he said:

Goodnight.

Hilton Head

Shadows of branches run like spokes
from the streetlight's yellow beam,
splayed against wet pavement.
An offshore breeze ascends the treetops,
whispers through the hotel window.

A woman writes at a lamp-lit desk:
a letter telling her lover to leave.
She reads it twice, folds and slides it
into a scented envelope. She licks the seal,
scrawls the address, and wonders how to send it.

She sets the letter on a stack of postcards,
crosses through the curtained doorway.
Her hands on the balcony railing, she kicks
off her shoes to stand in rain water, pooled,
her skin prickling in the pre-dawn air.

Showdown

When he struck that *High Noon* pose
to finger his six-shooters, itchy, I knew
right then there'd be no such thing as

meeting in the middle

right then I knew there'd be no such
thing as fingering his six-shooter, itchy
for that *High Noon* pose. Struck.

Ex Libris

I hold a book, borrowed
from you, its ivory slowly
yellowing; your dust filters
and settles on my hands.

When I reach the part where
the sweethearts kiss, a hair
from your head curls against
the page, black and gray.

I pry a nail beneath one end,
dislodge its rooted barb.
The hair slides toward my
rib and rests there, thin.

On the vellum leaf, the absent
filament makes its mark:
a curved impression, gentle
gorge, a sharpened scythe.

This novel ends on a dog-eared
sheet, your hair the only footnote.
The leather cover lies gilt-edged,
closed, the title there engraved.

Telegraph

Just before you write to me
I sense a gentle warning,
a bell on the breeze,
the smell before rain.

There will be dreams,
fogs of your face,
your mouth,
all lines of sorrow
running eight hundred miles to me
here in the wilderness.

I touch the mailbox.
My hand burns.
I know you're in there.

I'll tell you that
twenty sun-dappled deer
cross the yard. Two bucks
snap magnolia buds.
Their fawns wobble forward.
Their mothers' eyes glow.

Down the ravine
red foxes bound
through forest ferns.
Waterbugs mate atop
Green River, where catfish lie
along the murky bottom.

In the fields,
ditches fill with frogs
and backwater.
We hear the corn pop through,
breaking the yielding crust.
The leaves will twist up for rain.
Later comes the splitting hail.

We lose an acre or two.
We persist, laughing in the hammock,
or making strawberry pie.

You will read this,
smile,
and six months later
you will write again
to ask innocuous questions,
to reveal nothing at all.

New Linen

Thirty years ago, we laundered sheets
clipped to dry on cotton lines. Stretched
like sails, they snapped in sun-drenched day.
The heated parchment held us rapt, billowing.

Iris shoots pried the purpling sky.
The screened-in porch bore each new rain.
Briskets stewed in simmering herbs as tipsy
friends arrived and crowned the skirted table.

The curtain tore. In decades since, I wandered.
Bereft, I lay with men in futile hope,
in false fidelity. I wove the burial cloth,
pulled out loose threads, nocturnal fraying.

Now, we hem the ragged seam. Entwined
and tangled, wreathed and shrouded, wracked
by text and tender ache, we lie on linen,
bone on bone, on sheets we strip and wash.

Upon Learning of Your Death

Four months after the fact,
I open a note from your widow.
She writes of her sadness in sharing
the news of your slow demise.
I hunt the obituary archives,
read the passage limited there
to a few events, a too-brief summary:
your days on this earth.

It does not mention teaching me
to sail under bright skies on the Huron,
through the coves of Silver Lake.
It omits completely our sanding
the hull, brushing sealer on fiberglass,
mounting the mast, tying the whole
to the Rambler's roof, picnic lunches
in the back seat, ripe peaches and juice.

Nothing is said of walking in forests,
the pine needles softer than branches
foretold. No description is given of thirty
years' steadfastness, of meeting in secret,
of tickets and trains, the son I bore.
Only that you lived and breathed,
taught your courses, protested the wars,
married a woman

from whom you turned
in order to be held,
in whose arms you died
while saying my name.
The envelope lies unsealed,
its gilt-edged linen tattered,
the fold line grimy with fingering,
the glue flap pink with her lipstick.

Brigantine Island

All along the wet, onyx jetty
spumes of frothy sea water
slap and lick the rocks' ravines.
A lone man casts out his line,
slowly reels it in, not visible
to the woman who waits ashore
alone, restless in the fog.

Hollow

Long after each urgent cry,
impassioned plea
or silent prayer,
it comes down to this:
the call not returned,
the number forgotten,
the letter left to languish,
unopened, on the table.

Christmas Dance

The philosophy chair gave a Christmas party;
We were all invited to a dark wood mansion
on the top of the town's only hill.
Small candles flickered in gentle windows
trimmed in holly and red velvet.
Wearing our best manners and Sunday shoes,
we were served marzipan candies,
punch from silver bowls.

Out in the great room,
sofas huddled in a corner; thick
rugs rolled back, the oak floors gleaming.
A bluegrass band played wild, fast,
as whiskey pulled us to our feet.
We danced; we reeled.
Lamps and faces blurred; we could not
tell right from left.

A merciful waltz slowed us to breathing.
A man in a white shirt and tie rolled
up his sleeves, his hairy arms wiry.
He stood and drew his wife against
his chest, her head beneath his ear.
His arms crossed over her back.
Hip bones fused, their steps slow and sure,
I was ruined, ruined, waiting for a man like that.

Teaching Load

I was heavy with child then.
My office was topped by
tall windows so deep
I could climb right up,
read till I slept,
curled like my baby, safe.

I would unfurl then,
step down to the creaking, wide planks,
to the pool of streaming, amber light.
I'd kick off my shoes, sway in the rocker,
my bare feet golden in the wooden pond.

He came bustling down the hallway,
conjugating verbs, planning for class,
whistling. He stepped into my doorway,
arrested there. I paid no mind, my eyes closed,
dreaming. I heard his footsteps,
stealthy, soft. "May I?" he asked.

His fingers and palms rounded my belly.
His eyes grew wide and he whispered,
"All the secrets of the universe lie within."
He shuffled away, smiling, knowing
what to teach the students.

A Colleague's Death

You lie there, folded,
a flag or evening's flower.

Your bed softens,

    dandelion fluff
    cotton bolls, carded,
    combed, stretched flat
    like so many loving arms
    held out.

I pass your door;
press my palms to the cold window:
translucence.
Seen only now in shadow,
your edge grows dim
and fades.

For the Living

The sun slants hollow in the oak tree stand
where he and I once stood.
Shoots of mayapple have come and gone;
autumn is upon us.

Others have walked alongside us:
students, poets, lovers,
all eyes and ears as he swept his hand,
his pen,
across the creekbed of this living.

The path we took back to the barn
lay covered up in acorns.
Pressed into the soil by the sole of his shoe,
they took hold and climbed
in the shelter of the briar.

Hoes and plows, steel bits, a harness,
tether us to the corn crib.
Our words pile in like cobs.

The brittle husk, gone to dust,
scatters,
filtered and floating in the
air.

Widow Woman

The widow woman growls along in slow
motion to the front of the parlor.
She slumps into a chair, her hair
all up on her head like a beehive, her bottom
so big it hangs off the seat like
bread rising sideways.

We all have come for her husband's funeral:
the sorry flirts, ex-lovers, girlfriends,
all gathered up in the back of the room,
in the back seat of his car,
like dried flowers in clay vases.

Verna is the first one to speak.
"Well, I never. Onc't he promised to marry me
and carry me off in his Chevy to Asheville."
Laura and Mae, Mattie and Sue, armored in
push-up bras and violet perfume, sniff at Verna and claim,
"It was me, you fool. You ain't no-count."

One by one they brag
of secret dates at the Tastee Freeze,
the drive-in show, Jimmy Johnston's Skate-O-Rama,
flicking their trysts off some list like
worms from green tomatoes.

I recall wild honeysuckle beneath us.
Poems puffed from his lips
like adders in the brush.
I still have his hair in a locket,
his baby in my belly.

He Asks Me to Write of Him

I will sit down to write,
but not of you: only of
    the blue-black green of shadows,
    the way willow fronds sweep
    the grassy loins of earth;
of crocuses, spiders, their webs;
of the cracks and corners of this life,
yes.
Of you?
Perhaps later,
    when the thrashing of creek water
    grows quiet,
    when the turgid air clears.
Perhaps in the evening,
when flowers fold,
when the barn swallow rests
in her branches.

Moon on the Meadow

Moon on the meadow,
heather on the hill;
a green willow pond,
a loon's cry shrill.

Seeds on the stalk heads,
bluish blush on grass;
mice munch on berries,
then skitter up the pass.

Hens sit settled, clucking,
their sweet chicks gathered round;
in stalls the cows and ewe lambs
lie down on straw-gold ground.

A candle in the window,
hay bales in the loft;
cobs all in the corn crib,
leaves rustling soft.

Bats fly up, flapping
their pointy, peaked wings;
a baby cries down holler,
her sleepy grandma sings.

Moon on the meadow,
stars shining bright;
a farm out in the valley,
her grandpa's sweet *Goodnight*.

Train Window

Two blue herons,
the rock-hemmed shore;
slow, steady swoop:
wing over water.

At Water's Edge

I. Heron

And as she plunges,
the wind ruffles blue feathers;
one fish leaps for joy.

II. Pools

When the blue lagoon
infused them with its orchids,
they swam into night.

Kentucky Tomato

My friend, I hunger
for the fruits of your labor.
I miss your kitchen conversation,
those mugs of thick milk,
yellow curtains, garden flowers,
terra cotta tiles.

I see your hands: long fingers
bend to cradle a tomato.
They dripped, the seeds strewn
across lean knuckles, brown
lines in skin, white nails;
their half-moons glistened.
You sliced sideways, the knife sharp:
red slabs slid to the chilled white plate.

We sat together, laughing.
Our stories, our dreams
unfurled like husks,
the kernels cutting through.

Drive

   I.   They will build these roads
      against slope of hill,
      over creekbeds.
      Concrete gaps shift, laughing.
      I drive along in eerie fog.

  II.   A groundhog's chunky body
      grinds a slow squash.
      My right tire spins blood.

 III.   That frosty afternoon,
      two fat boys in suspenders
      jump off the school bus and run.
      Their father waits, waving,
      their ears bent under hats with flaps.
      Morning glories wither on the porch.

      He waves and waves.

Penobscot Bay Lament

In coastal Maine, this land
of harbor, seaport,
widows' walks,
I sit in the rocker,
look out across the bay.

The silent, rolling seals, a whale;
all manner of life teems
beyond the rocky shore.

Ice glistens at the tips.
Fingers of frozen water
reach into inlets and coves
like the ghosts of
your dead father,
your old lover,
your ancient past,
reclaimed.

A fog of sleet rises above the bed,
my body a tombstone in the closed
cemetery: two feet of snow,
and more predicted.

Museum of Fine Arts: Boston

Vincent Van Gogh

It's just that I crave
these thick paintings,
strokes of brush,
nail, fingerslab, oil:
the breaking, liquid light.

Käthe Kollwitz

Tender figures,
bronze lovers croon.
He holds her upturned head.
Her eyes close.

Auguste Renoir

Dancers at Bougival press
before me.
Her bonnet, flaming tangerine,
a cream cloud of dress, flowing.
His blue shirt, pants, black boots
planted, firm.
Eyes hidden under hat,
the pale skin of a reddish man.
Her caution, his desire.
She looks away;
his mouth draws near.
Her waist relents;
his neck grows taut.
He will ask;
she will agree.

Henri Matisse

I walked another floor while
daylight fell;
dark clouds embraced
the night's soft lawn.
Bright cut-outs blue against
a string quartet.
Women leapt through holes
in space, their hearts
a shining throb.
On the marble bench
my thighs grazed
the naked notes.

Exit

Three kids bang a loud
piano, their voices
racked with glass.
A woman's stiletto heels
hammer the clacking floor.
Security says it's closing
time. Impressionist blurs
slide down the thin wall,
creep along the floor,
bind my ankles.
Halted, haunted,
bare fingers grasp
the hollow air.
You are not here.

Michigan

I live now in Virginia,
where winter sheets the land,
a light jacket of dim chill.
This is not true winter,
not like in Michigan,
where snows covered our doors and Papa
climbed the roof to dig us out.
We tunneled under frozen igloos, laughing:
the delight of a warm and secret place.

I climbed the picnic table at night,
a snowbound, wooly mammoth,
lay on my back and looked up.
The northern lights blazed in an
ageless arc of swirl and vapor.
I ached to be taken up, dissolved:
particles of radiance.

Now, I hear arbutus rustling,
the bumping of the logs,
skates scraping on ice.
I smell spiced cider,
pine forests,
frozen air.
I turn
within and within and within,
finding the long way home.

San Francisco

I walk in Muir forest
amid the fallen redwoods.
Shoots of new trees reach
into the vapory mist.
I press my palms to the wind of our parting.

The wind presses back.
It is then that the throat thickens,
closes. No words can rise to push
against the redwood stand,
the falling, gilded light.

You are as faithful as shifting clouds,
as rusting leaves.

Cabbie

In a city phone booth,
   cracked glass
   urine ice floor
   a wino's stain
   a dangling receiver
   Susie . . . wow! TR-8-0163
   and
   For a real good time
   or even
   Lola loves Linda

a cabbie
   deliverer of bodies
   traffic slow hour rush
   city nights
stops to call out,
finds a grimy dime.

He spits on it,
   rubs it against a chamois shirt.
   Mercury's fine curls appear,
   the date, *In God We*
   "Trust thyself," Emerson said.
   Where should we look but within?

He pockets the shiny coin,
   hangs up the receiver.
   He has searched their eyes
   in rearview mirrors,
   looked for the low spark
   of another soul, lost and lonely.

He rides out to the airport
    to retrieve a lady in blue
    whistling, "Bess, you is my woman."
He has combed his hair slimy,
    will wait all night at the gate
    for the cargo that neverneverlands.

Flight to India

Above the Mediterranean,
toward the Arabian Sea,
through low banks of clouds,
the sun sets in the west;
its long rays stretch,
fingers of fading light.

From Istanbul to Bombay,
the wails of mullahs rise:
tambourines and tablas,
the imam's eerie cry.

Women in flowing robes,
secret jewels, veiled eyes flashing.
Orchids in the Agra, tangerines,
pomegranates, dates and figs,
goats' heads, severed.
I'm lost and drowning.

A bony finger points the way
to yearning's cobbled path:
the petals and the peasant,
patchouli and myrrh,
dung and marigold,
jasmine bowers.

Beloved, I shall return to tell you these things.

Kashmiri Houseboat

In a dark river flowing,
encircling the earth,
your tropical genitals float in my dream,
an island nation of bougainvillea:
male mynah birds calling.

Wrapped in orchid desire,
I lounge poolside and sip cloudy
drinks from a tall, lazy glass,
a paper umbrella perched on its rim,
salt lime edging my lips.

Two Peonies

A crystal vase,
slender leaves.

Heads heavy on
tendril stalks,
two peonies bloom,
their fluted edges
flail, vivid, white.
Stark pink centers
billow, their yellow pistils
protrude.

Thaw in Karnataka

Just before you come to me
in this depth of winter melt,
the sluice overflows,
roof dams run.
I have heard your voice,
a rushing wind, cypress knots.

Soon I will see
the underbellies of leaves,
the banyan trees,
their silver throats,
your face—in its lined,
sandy beaches,
I'll yield to thaw,
to chaos,
calm.

And there, in the blue/black shadow,
in fern-laden loam,
jacks-in-the-pulpit rise,
cattails,
jimson weed and
spores, airborne;
dandelion,
wild mustard:
these fields,
these rivers,
this air.

India: Step

Because I chirped *hello*, I startled
Usha's father. He fell the full length
of twelve marble steps. I stood above
the foyer, watched as each bony joint,
the crane-like skull, struck pink stone.

Usha cried out, bent to him, dabbed
with a corner of her cotton pallu.
Blood bloomed into her sari's hem,
spread across the glistening tiles.
Slowly he rose, shaken, alive.

If only I could call them back,
withdraw my good intentions, restore
the railing to his hand, set down the out-
stretched foot. Years later, I still see
the midstride hope: safe landing.

Banyan Haiku

Out of these thoughts
a bird lit on your shoulder.
She whispered in your ear.

Taj Mahal

Like a stalk of light, your hand
rests on the wall beside me.
You lean toward me. I look
away; a thin line of longing
breaks as you laugh,
your voice a depth of mahogany.

You reach into your basket,
pin jasmine in my hair.
My sari, white as marble—
orchids broil in the heat.
Barefoot in the garden,
your eyes rise to meet my gaze.

The Last Note

On the final leg of a four-month tour,
our weary band of Celtic musicians
(ragged singers, pipers, hoodlums, clowns)
straggles into a coastal town, humming.
We open our beds and sleep for two days.

We wake, stretch, dress, and walk
to Donovan's Pub. Steaming bowls of potatoes,
red cabbage, biscuits and cream,
coffee strong enough to startle the dead,
appear before us, refracted in stained glass windows.

"A wee nip for luck," we say. "Saints
be praised." We hoist a few, our eyes
then drawn to Eugene's boyhood portrait,
hung above the door, encircled in black crepe.
We stand and joke, our shoes against the rail.

It is Galway in July. A damp crowd clusters
on the town hall steps clutching tickets for
that night's show. When we leave the bar,
it is Liam's head they see first, he being tallest.
A cheer goes up. Handshakes all around.

Baskets of jam and bread, tatters of poems,
babies to hold and cluck over. One woman
sighs, "It's a shame about Eugene. Who'll play
the fiddle now he's dead and gone?"
"O'Domnhail," I say. "Good, but not the same."

At seven we tune: bouzoukis, citterns, pipes, and flutes.
Painted bodhrans rest at the ready. In regal
stride, the piper leads us past ticketmen,
down the aisle, up the creaky steps, the people in
a roar: we climb the wooden stage.

We play and sing. Small rivulets of sweat
run down our backs, run under our ribs:
wild jigs and reels, ballads, slow airs,
lullabies and laments 'til someone calls out,
"Play one of Eugene's!"

We swallow. Our throats tighten. I look at
the roof line and steel myself for singing.
We make it halfway through his well-known dirge:
E'en the Throes of Death Shall Not Part Us.
But one by one we falter.   (83

Christy sets his wood flute down.
The pipes groan to silence. Davvy tries
to push the words through tears.
His breathing heaves, catches his ragged
grief. One by one we stop.

Then, from out of the high balcony,
like wind rustling through barley,
a bit of melody lifts, the faint words
far off at first, then gathering strength
as people stand, one here, more there.

Row after row they rise in waves,
two thousand Irishmen singing, softly,
"Somewhere beyond the bower,

my true love waits for me. No death
can ever part us, throughout eternity."

In four-part, a capella harmony,
their voices thrum. When the last note
dies down, a full minute passes.
Then comes applause,
raining like thunder.

Walloon Lake

I return to the north country,
to the land of lakes and loons,
to tethered boats that bob and wait.
Gulls screech along the pebbled shore;
ropes coil around split pilings.

I return to brushy pine trees,
their needled spires, resin, tar.
Against their trunks pale birch
groves stand; their tentative skins
peeled and curled, small wounds exposed.

I return to the pier of my childhood,
as if my lines still lie along the mast,
as if my parents' light is on,
as if a lover will appear in a second
story window and call my name.

A hawk rises up, nesting threads
clutched and dangling in her talons.

Swimming in the Nude

I swim, sleek as a seal,
cold in the midnight lake.
Water runs through my hair,
turns, rushes past my shoulders,
pools in the depths of my hips,
cascades along my tickling legs.

I lunge deeper into blackness,
shed skins of loss, of earthbound
woe. I skim below the bristling waves,
outrace their ebb and swell. I mourn
our lack of gill, break surface, breathe:
the shocking air. I float and drift.

A dome of stars caps wet horizons;
its bright illusion braces me. I swim
as if slight shifts in fin or tail will
set new courses. I do not see
an anchored boat. I can't touch bottom.
There is no shore. I smile and dive again.

Edge

I will live at the edge of the land
where the sea greets the sky:
an endless gray horizon.

I will shed this city like snakeskin,
misspent debris,
this driftwood of a life.

The sun lays down its liquid
tongue of flame on an ocean valley;
timeless waves break against the
fevered coast of all thought.

I will walk among blanched bones,
froth and foam, beach tar, spume,
the rock-hewn coast;
a solitary seagull cries
an echo of my yearning.

The lighthouse beacon pulls me into harbor.
My home awaits me: a cobbled hearth,
slate floors, windows without glass;
a granite path along the shore road.

The heart brought to solitude
returns to itself.
I am leaving in the morning.
I will not look back.

Consider:

the big bang,
constellations beyond
swirling vapor,
atomic life,
threads of carbon
all
motion-bound.

Or:
lily-of-the-valley,
seed pod, cell,

the propagating impulse.

Lovers embrace
in the physics of skin,
magnetic push and pull,
our universal need,
that moment both
zenith
and grave.

Andre Agassi, 36, Holds On to Win

"The old man," they call him. After icing
spasms, he limps to the net, cortisone-infused,
battling a boy half his age. He gathers himself,
rallies through tie breakers, deuce; he gains
the advantage, pushes past grinding pain,
conquers sudden death in five straight sets.

That's one miracle.
Here's the other.

The crowd of twenty-three thousand cheers each point,
each game, rising to its feet, roaring, clapping,
its own mortality realized, defeated, in a singular man
who, at 12:38 A.M., sets down his racket,
wipes his gleaming head, waves back, and lifts
the trophy for all the frenzied fans to see.

Watching the Weatherman

I recall third-grade fire drills,
or riding the pickup's bumper,
careening down the dark and wild
streets of youth, shining
with reckless indifference.

Then, my mother's prayers seemed
incoherent mutterings.

How have I come to be so cautious?

I lock my doors, bless my children,
worry when tornadoes threaten.

Once I leaped from puddle to puddle.
Water crawled up my ankles, soaked
the pants Mama so carefully ironed
while watching the weatherman.

Haze

On this hot day
    a plume of heat
    drizzles
    off the asphalt.

Arms raised,
    my naked children,
    brown, thirsty flowers,
    run in sprinkler rain.

They spray me.
    Goose bumps
    rise, shocked
    hairs erect.

Clothes on the line
    crackle;
    even the plush towels
    drop hard as boards.

Ice in our lemonade
    dissolves before
    we drink. Our hands
    slip on the glass.

Our bodies
    stick. We hang,
    cracked
    in the haze.

Kodak Moments

The closets needed cleaning, especially the bureau drawer,
the one with all the photos, so I started making piles
according to year or guessed-at year but then I thought
I'd arrange by person, sort of a daughter no. 1 pile and then sons
no. 1, no. 2, daughter no. 2, then sons 3 and 4, et cetera,
but there were so many shots of all of you together
and I didn't want any cutting going on.

So then I used the thematic approach, all of the pumpkin
and costume prints or Christmas or the picnic
every year at Grandpa's but then I sorted
by birthdays, graduations, marriages, the births
of the next generation. But then who should get which
and what if there weren't enough to go around
all six of you and who might feel left out and hurt?

So then I hit on the idea of just grabbing an assorted
bundle and putting them into one scrapbook,
then another handful and another book and so on
until I had filled six books and had used up all
the pictures but for the few I wanted to sprinkle around the
house and sure enough, it worked out fine.
Here they are. Hope you like them.

The Zen of Cleaning Glasses

I bathe my glasses,
rub their round lenses
with soap, green liquid,
under hot water.
I take time,
as in washing my baby,
slowly reaching suds
to the crevice behind her ear,
each fold of fat thigh,
between each toe.
I rinse them,
the bubbles sheeting away.
I dry them,
patting with a dimpled paper towel,
moisture absorbed.
I put them on,
their stems still warm,
tortoise-shell, necessary,
framed light.

Matthew

Of all my six children,
one freckle-faced wonder
remains a mother's mystery.
How is it he still lives?
This cat with six lives left
and counting . . .

Born with a hole in his heart,
brain surgery at five,
a drive-by shooting at seven.

In April he ventured to the creek,
lusty with spring, to frolic in poison sumac.
In class, he caught pinkeye, head lice.
A broken nose followed
the ruptured appendix.
The local nurses know him by name.

The ER doctor, a neighbor,
while showering and shaving her legs,
saw something flitting by in the
skylight window. While reaching
for a towel, she saw my son
in the top of a thirty-foot spruce,
swaying in the wind, yelling,
"Hey, Doc!"

I would bind him to the couch,
shackle him, ball and chain,
the weight of a mother's crushing love.

Yet he is his unpliable own.
Fate within his wiry frame,
my heart in his hand,
he bolts out the door,
long, lean,
laughing.

Gabriel

In a high school cafeteria
walled in gray tile, fluorescent lights,
industrial columns every sixteen feet,
my teenaged son warms up
for the ensemble competition.
He plays trombone in a brass quartet.
He will be called before the judge who hides,
unknown, behind the burlap screen.

Dripping with hormones,
pimply-faced and orthodontically armored,
they polish their horns.
They tune the sharps and flats.
They play practice runs, a discordant, clamoring shrill.
My boy says, "Let's try that again."
Their feet thrum to an exact beat.
Their eyes narrow, nailing notes to the page.
Their throats swell; they purse their lips.
The *Brandenburg Concerto* rises, lush,
harmonious, unbelievable,
this miracle flung against school walls.

After his judging my son emerges, flushed.
I open his car door, dust off his seat.
He is gleaming, this boy,
this god, who
needs no ride home.

Snowboard 101: My Four Sons

At the ski slope a gaggle
of teenaged boys hops off the lift,
shifts around the bend,
positioned, edgy:
the downhill slide.

One falls, the youngest.
Embarrassed in awkward grace,
unsure, he calls out,
a pup in the wolfpack.
He thinks they will sneer,
rush past him, fly on,
easy in long-legged confidence.

As they approach his ruined ride,
his elders bow down.
Shoulders hit the banks.
Legs go airborne, hips thud hard,
board attached to boot.
Jumbled limbs jangle to stillness.

I hear them laughing, these
men of snow and ice.
As they stand in blue air,
they offer open hands,
raise up
the boy beneath.

Bone

Out of the boy's left thigh
a bloody, bleached shard of bone.
Streaked, torn shreds of muscle:
the jagged joint, the marbled knob.

Guest Room

At the airport, my son
and I wait in line. It is 5 A.M.
We attempt small pleasantries, but he is leaving.
He shoulders a backpack, shuffles his feet,
clutches a ticket and a thrumming need to fly.
Wearing fatigues and berets, soldiers grasp
the barrels of loaded rifles, patrol
the sprawling horde that winds
and tangles down the dim concourse.

Some people shove, several babies cry.
My son just smiles and asks if I remember:
the long way home. I turn a page
in the novel I am reading.
He checks his baggage, hugs me goodbye.
Passing through security, he turns back to wave.
His head disappears in the fading throng.
Driving back, I listen to the news,
check all my rearview mirrors.

Standing at the hotel window,
I watch plane after plane lift into
the burgeoning dawn.
Six stories down, a jogger braves the circling path.
Autumn leaves swirl around her feet.
Morning fog rises off the tree-lined river;
I hear the cries of geese.
From rusting bracken, a woodland duck
ascends the current and is gone from me.

Daughters

Lovely rosebud lips,
creamy skin of breast-fed babe,
downy fur and crinkled brow,
balled-up fists, unfurling.
Walking the floor.

Teething rings, finger paint,
dolls and plush stuffed toys.
"No!" and endless hissy fits,
baths and lullabies, pajamas.
Walking the floor.

Dating, hiding, rules unheeded,
locked diaries, unruly boys,
fierce hatred, short hemlines.
Past time to be in. Smoking.
Walking the floor.

Packing to leave for
college, a job, that new love,
freedom, overdrawn checking
accounts, too many bills.
Walking the floor.

But then comes that phone call:
realization, apology, request,
all rolled into one weepy
sentence. I ease your distress,
walking the floor.

One Young Wife's Tale

O my husband,
waving the gun,
your eyes roll:
     a horse bolts
     the barbed fence,
     the end of pasture.
And the children scream,
clutching my legs.
We panic for exits.
     One shimmies out the window,
     runs to the neighbors,
     calls the police.
Their nightmares boom thunder,
crack sidewalk cement.
From the railed bed,
you rise to scream,
buckling, ripping
tubes from veined arms.
The nurse cradles my elbow,
croons into my ear,
bulldozes me gently out the door.

The Children and I Shall Meet Again

This son grows tall and he grows
habits of mind and bearing and he grows
away from me until all I am to him
is a memory in the wind.
If I'm lucky, he'll still speak
to me, but if I'm not, he'll flick
me like so much ash off the tip
of his lit escape.

I miss him, even his subtle cruelties.
The children still at home plot
their time remaining, bound
and aloof, affectionate, chafing under
the rib of overbearing genetics.
I hear them now, singing like sirens,
their charted destinies flung
toward death's door.

I am like them, for when I finally
leaf and flower, depart this house,
its hidden truths thick as walls,
free of briars and thorns,
of my marital mistake, I will run
into the great wide blue
at a galloping pace; we will climb down
the walls on knotted sheets.

Rx: Mother and Children

Aching	backs muscles joints memory.
Twisted	knees shoulders points of view.
Swollen	tendons sinews ankles pride.
Pierced	eardrums earlobes earaches silence.
Broken	noses toes one skull hearts.
Punctured	palms soles lungs well-being.
Severed	nails fingertips ligaments contact.
Apply	iodine ointment bandage splint cast love.
Brace	yourself.
Push	them out.
Wrap	their wounds.
Admit	defeat.
Prognosis	they'll live.

Sewanee Haiku

I raise the shade, hail
a new day. Two deer appear
beyond my window.

The Workshop Poet

enters the room in a lethargic stride.
He is late. His glasses ride the ridge
of his nose. A slash of bone,
plateau of cheek. Grizzled hairs
gnaw at his nape. His silver mane.
A jacket so wrinkled it curls
above his skeletal hips. He shuffles
the poems like dead leaves.

Tapered fingers drum as he contemplates
bad work. Old, befuddled yet brilliant,
he will drink tonight, no breathless girl
beside him. New poets irritate, their
pointless, whining emotion. He looks
at us, begins to speak, then waves his
glasses toward the stained glass window.
He staggers to his feet and saunters out.

Reprieve

At eighty-one, the weary
poet lies asleep, his
aching bones long dry.
The clock strikes two.

His virgin student creeps
along the corridor,
hears his ragged breath,
tries the clacking doorknob.

He stirs and sits upright;
her dress spills moonlight,
blue wildflowers grasped
and falling from her hands.

Assignment

A flurry of snow-blind
notions fills your head.
A line, an image.
Grab one.
Place it between
white sheets.
Write
the tale of yearning,
of winsome youth,
of angst and need
for solitude,
of ice upon branches.
Describe slow steps
toward fruition,
then just try to ignore
death's mangled hand
upon your shoulder.

In Fog

In fog the sadness rises
  and will not take its leave.

I walk the sloping campus
  past the arching bower.

Wetness plods to earth,
  from fingertips of pine

to pebbled walkway; soon I
  grow as small and mottled,

smooth and pale as pea-sized
  gravel on the path.

In my room, I prop
  the windows up with books.

I write a while, brood,
  then stop to watch the wind.

Thunder sounds, forewarns,
  as arrowed birds take cover.

Soft rains fall
  then tear the yielding trees.

I step out to breathe
  the raw and drenching sky.

The deluge pounds against
    slated courtyard roofs.

Spilling itself, the storm
    abates to steady downfall,

persists till dusk arrives,
    plush with evening's shadow.

Lake Cheston

I walk the forest, needle-floored,
cross the grassy plain, slope down
to cattails, coves, an inlet, sand:
the silver, velvet lake. The sun,
descending, warms the water's mantle.

Laced by treetops,
evening's light lingers.

Swarms of swallows rise and fall,
lift and plunge, break the bronzing
surface. Arrowed wings taper,
fan like flukes. Birds lunge and snap,
feast: green mayflies glide, leave

foot-long wakes,
feather-thin, metallic.

Alone, not lost, I swim out, far.
The nesting swallows whistle, sing,
call home the darkening dusk.
I drift to shore and sit, chest-deep.
I wonder if you think of me.

One by one,
faint stars appear.

Lake Cheston in the Rain

I slowly swim my crocodile crawl;
small ebbs break the bridge of my nose.
Not moving the surface and leaving no wake,
I see black clouds looming.
A mantle of mist descends from pines,
hovers near the obsidian surface.
Steam rises off the lake; it lingers as
the air grows frigid.

A drop hits my head. One splatters here,
another, there. A rapid crescendo swells
till the downpour opens, torrential.
Rain pummels the water. Liquid
craters splay; their centers shoot upward
into pips. As I swim farther out,
rough and splashing dimples pock
the fog-enshrouded horizon.

I wrongly thought the birds would flee,
take cover from deluge. I watch them dive
and playfully swerve, riding out the day's
provision, its beneficence. I turn onto my back
to float downstream, eyes closed. Raindrops
pelt my face and chest, stinging, sharp,
as friends yelp from shore,
frantic, running for the car.

Southern Landscape

A yellow bowl of blackberries,
a hydrangea blue plate,
white linen napkins.

A woman in a cotton dress
leans against a kitchen chair's
red oilcloth padding.

The wind off the bayou
skims her skin fine
as a cedar's barbed needles.

It really is this simple:
cool water to drink,
a screen in the window,

air enough to breathe.

For Sale

Looking for a man is like selling my house,
so I shore up my floor joists,
spackle my cracks, install
an alarm on my sump pump.
I paint, using neutral colors,
resurface the cabinets.

Then I advertise, tell a few small lies:
"Cozy, charming bungalow!
Solid foundation! Energy-efficient!
Must see! Why rent when you can own?"
There's no down payment on this fixer-upper,
this handyman special.

Months go by without a nibble.
I check local sales, comparable values.
Sunken living room, cathedral ceilings:
I reduce my price. After all,
it's a thirty-year mortgage, fixed,
and there's interest to pay.

A Woman's Want

stalks the city
crawls through vents
drips down
plumbing, steals
into an office
crystallizes on
a keyboard.
Her desire slides
under doorways
seeps into carpet
rises on humidity
flies from exhaust
fans, paces all
night. Her need
slithers
parks in a bar
looks around
locks in on one
willing victim
orders straight
up, neat.

Cape Cod

From up here
   on the dune
   the sea looms ominous,
   midnight blue.
Breaking waves roil against
   the quiet coast, laced
   with the froth
   of lost wishes.

Tossed over the brine
   like shrimpers' nets,
   hooked, torn, bleeding,
   our baited bits of flesh,
we cast out our yearning,
   wondering who or what
   will come
   reeling in.

Proposal

If we should touch beneath the table,
flushing up surprised, rare birds
lifting, stealthy, under skin,
in what barbed moment might we meet?

If I should take your offered hand,
lined and brown, slow to touch,
to thresh and hone my cheek's parched heat,
what chance might soar in these bright days?

If you should leave before the birds
have plundered all from craggy banks,
before the rushing creeks recede,
what dark, soft rain could wash me clean?

Falling Leaves

Along the red brick walk, my back against an oak,
I watch the students run to class, their backpacks full,
their faces bright for teacher talk. Ivied buildings,
limestone, marble, spiral stairwells, flags of many
nations mark this place, this time, these days away
from you. Late magnolias, glossy foliage, lure me
out from work, their saucer blossoms sweet in air.
I wonder if you think of me. In fall, the earth
will turn, the sun slant low. In your yellow kitchen,
you wait to hear from me. I rise to write new poems.
Hayrides. Pumpkin patch. Cider. Rusting leaves.
The crisp night breeze will waken us. Pull the covers
closer, dear. I'll lay my head upon your chest.
Winter's coming soon: no time to sleep alone.

Roxbury Mill

Fireflies signal across the river.
Their ebbing code calls me
out on a roofline deck
above the concrete dam.

Rushing sheets of water slide,
crash down the rocks' ravine,
cascade and calmly gather, full:
the silver moon, the mill pond's glass.

A heron rises, lifts away
from nest and eddy; suspended,
wingspan steady, her feathers billow.
She hovers in the restless breeze.

The river, bridling the lazy bank,
rolls along; its soft waves break.
The heron swoops through branch and briar:
the moonlit bay, the waiting ocean.

Waterrock Knob

My finger traced the arced forest
of his arm, from wrist to inner plain.
Dense hairs met and merged in
the dovetailed valley, the crook of his elbow
smooth and bare as a mountain bald
and I wanted to live there forever.

Slant Cinquain

Slim, bare
treetops laced the
hidden moon, our sky a
fog no sun could break; we talked till
birds called.

Blender

Ingredients:

    one B movie
    two glasses Merlot
    two fifty-somethings
    one six-year drought.

Add:

    the question
    test results
    one condom.

Mix
Swirl
Swizzle
Chop
Grate
Shred

Serve:

    on the rocks
    over easy
    sunny side up.

The Love Zone ABCs: A Romance

Angular and agile,
a babe unbridled,
Corinna Crowe
decided to dine
early and eat at
Frank's Fine Foods.
She gamely glanced at goulash,
hash browns, ham,
when Ivan the itinerant iterated a
jocular joust,
kinky, kinetic,
laced with lewd
meaning. "My monkey," she moaned.
Nudging nearer, she noticed
his open and opulent
pocket. Pert pencils perched,
quartered near his quaking,
rakish ribs.
Steamy and smarmy,
the tart turned to
utter her ultimatum.
Villainous vixen, Corinna
whet her wants,
exhaled excitedly and exhorted him to ecstasy.
She yowled "Yes! Yes!"
zesty, zealous, zoned.

Slope

Somewhere on a mountaintop,
a woman moves across a window.
In frosted panes of glass,
fireplace flames and candles flicker,
their glow as steady as wandering
fog above bare branches.

Beyond the snow-covered ridge,
crest upon crest of buckled earth beckons.
She lifts the sash, washed in icy air.
The bite of cedar fern falls on her tongue,
brushes and braces the fevered skin.
His woodsmoke fades as she lingers,

their bed a gaping linen maw;
She traces his impression.
A longing rises up,
sudden as a red-tailed hawk,
deep as rock and ravine.
She turns, his name on her lips.

The Moon

The moon sidles low.
Its luminous sighs sling shadows on a wall.
Venetian blinds, three ferns,
a woman's hair waves down like leaves.
Across the lake,
the campfires burn, small barn owls coo
along the broken cliffs.

Sycamores gleam,
their mottled whiteness livid.
Spruce berries ripen
and burst, staining the rocks down
to the water's edge.
The moon, in the water's mouth,
ripples away.

In this long hour you must be
restless, alone, yet turning,
resistant. Unfurl.
The skies will stroke
your hair. The wind will kiss
your palms, leave sweet curry on your tongue.
The moon will wait for you.

Vine

Some lovers lay their passion
    like touch-me-nots
    on softest down.
Others tend their one-night love
    like brief-blooming cereus,
    quick moonflowers.

My love,
I am a creeping vine,
a weed, ever-flowering.
I will press into your crannies,
into each sidewalk crack,
my tendrils in your picket hair.

I will snake across your shoulders,
slither deep into your palms,
grow pods between your fingers.
I will climb your rooted ankles,
ascend the thigh-high arbor to
circle, circle the lurid pistil.

Spring Rain

A chilled fog rises
in the predawn hour
to beat back sleep.

At the dripping window
I look across the yard,
the treetops, to the same

sky under whose sheet
you lie sleeping. I wonder
if you are curled or sprawled,

if your wool socks sag,
if your arm is crooked
beneath an empty pillow.

I sit at the night window,
my chin in my hand,
the teacup heavy in my lap:

in the spring garden
ferns unfurl, their frothy
leaves black with spores.

Earth Science

They met behind the hanging maps
to cram for their exams, a library
lamp their only compass rose.
She studied skin geography,
all his global boundaries, setting
warm fronts, scale and key.
Sounding sea depths, grottoes,
canyons, they marked the brushy forests,
noted latitude and longitude.
To chart her floating islands,
he moved closer to her shelf.
On the brimming edge of fault lines,
lost in tropical disturbance,
plates collided, vast, tectonic.
After continental drift,
once the jet stream had receded
from the plateaus and the plains,
they contemplated clouds.

Lazy Sunday Morning

On lazy Sunday morning
we make love,
our bed a haphazard junkyard,
spilled newspapers, dry coffee cups.
We rise and dress:
you braid my hair.

We walk the long, easy block
from church—
where cherubs scratch their necks and
Henry sings off-key, too loud—
to deli, where Mrs. Goldfarb
winks at you and places
one extra blintz on your plate.

Hindman Poetry Reading

An argyle sweater man in silver spectacles
sits shoulder-to-chin with a pink
linen lady in champagne hair.
They listen to me and nod,
smiles gathering, the corners of their eyes
frayed by years of leaning toward
one another.
They breathe in unison.

We will grow old like this:
no need for word or argument.
A settled peace will filter down like
sunlight on the windowsill.

Trellis

Along the trail's rock wall,
pools of white petals flutter
against gray and pitted stone;
they scatter across my path,
lifted by the morning breeze.
I remove my shoes and step
into the frilled bouquet,
the wind-blown eyelet.

As a girl, I dreamed of lilacs
strewn along the wedding aisle
by naiads dressed in pink. In India,
jasmine bowers hung from archways.
I clipped small cuttings to wear in
my hair, the buds moist and soft.

When I returned, I paused
beneath a cherry tree near
its end of season. As I looked up,
the thinning boughs released
a shower of last leavings:
petals brushed my skin.

Now I see a lover in the garden,
on his knees, a trowel in hand,
planting rose bushes. They will
climb the woven trellis, leaf
and flower, their thorns too few
to matter. These petals will fall
and cushion our walk, scudding
in the wind's swift insistence.

Penance

Each time I doubt, a tall glass shatters.
My face refracted in the glittering shards,
fragments fall, cutting my feet.
Red droplets rise to the surface of skin.

When fear overwhelms, I run from you,
grow lost as a void. The starless night,
stretched past the known, turns back
to mock, to nullify pride.

Each time I go, each time I rip the seam
that binds, whole worlds implode.
Nothing sweet to look upon remains:
no sun, no moon, no rapt eyes shining.

David

How real he looks, standing there
in stony silence, anatomically correct,
poised as if to escape pushy guards
and sweaty tourists snapping away.
I imagine sidling up to kiss him,
planting a fat one on those lovely lips.
How would it feel against those pecs?
(Not to mention . . .) I'll never know.

What if he ran away, or hopped a flight
to watch the World Cups? Who'd swarm
him then? Surely footie fans would admire
his energy, raw athleticism. That height!
Would hairdressers swoon for those curls?
He should cut his toenails and think about
water retention. Doves peck at his earlobes;
their waste runs down his neck.

The Bells of Santa Croce

The morning air warms to rouse small birds.
Their fluttering stirs leaves. A twig falls; two
squirrels scatter. The sun turns to me as bells
invite the widows of Santa Croce to prayer.

One by one, Vespas whirr across the piazza.
Hotel waiters tie aprons and stroll to work.
My room overlooks the terrace; hibiscus in pots,
honeysuckle, climb cracked walls and shutters.

I sit to write, the Arno glinting beyond trees.
Last night's Chianti, sipped from a paper cup,
tastes bitter now. I know you're home, packing,
a one-way ticket nestled in your pocket.

New travel awaits us, in separate compartments,
you to the north country; I'll keep the home fires
ashen. *Bon voyage* we'll say, and mean it,
our sad smiles not completely forced.

My carry-on breaks, a zipper tooth missing.
There's news of a taxi strike and World Cup scores.
I'm grateful for distraction, for café con latte.
Discovery will launch, the weather notwithstanding.

Orthodoxy

In a Tuscan shul, I heard the old men singing psalms.
Behind the gated grillwork, women bound by Torah
gathered kids and stood for prayer.

On arching walls, mosaic Stars of David mildewed,
crumbling through the plaster. Horsehair cushions, threadbare,
lined the walnut chairs in rows.

Above the dome, through strips of colored glass, the sun
cast down its splayed prisms, spangling kippot, woolen
shawls. In solitary moment,

in a bid for new redemption, I took off
his ring, the long engagement canceled. It pulled
away, reluctant, stubborn fingers

used to company. A thin line left a mark.
When service ended, I walked down the marble steps;
the rabbi saw and wept with me.

Wheat Fields

Let me live just long enough
to cut and reap my former sorrows,
to gather up their kernels, smooth;
to bless and cast them once, anew,
as shimmering fields: the waving fronds,
a glancing sun, their webbed roots
loving moisture in the loam.

Bag of Rings

I open the jewelry drawer,
gather tinkling gemstones:
gold and silver, platinum
bands, antiques. Emerald
prisms in diamond halos
refract new morning light.

I find a gray silk pouch,
its maroon ribbon smooth
and knotted at both ends.
Twelve rings slide down the sac,
clink against each other,
settle in nestled metallurgy.

"Too bad," I say. No lover
lasted long enough to forge
a bond, no mounting worth
its keeping. These baubles' sale
will buy a chair, a wicker
rocker, flowered cushions.

Sail

I head out in this harbor
anchoring landmarks:
a gap in the trees,
two buoys off the dock.
A slow bell clangs.
Gray waves lap against the bow.

The sail conceives the wind,
bellows, grows taut.
Leaning over the edge,
I once raced and flew,
and won or lost on a chance—
that balance between gravity and flight.

Content now to drift,
the slack sail flaps.
Holding the line,
I tack upstream.

E. Atlantic

We walk the mile from inn to market.
A man from Jamaica grins and cuts up
chicken left to turn on the spit for hours.
We put strawberries in the cart, herbed
cheese for baguettes, orange juice and greens.
We pay the girl in pink barrettes, her hair
splayed like palm fronds fanning the breeze.

Back in the room, we lick our fingers,
love each other in a world where everything
perishes, even as it feeds.

Delray

In the things that count
we share like minds, equal
as two shore birds who pull
and shred a bit of fish.
Contending, we feed each other.

In smaller matters,
we rub, then merge
like grains of sand.
In friction, we grow
round and smooth

as sea glass, translucent,
the edges gone to aqua disks
as currents crave the waiting
beach in crawling waves,
froth-filled.

Rite of Purification

Your hands, brown light,
find small birds in my body
and illuminate them.

Your mouth, sweet fastener,
clings to wet rocks, moss,
sea creatures, licorice ferns.

In the boggy garden,
a dark morel lifts,
silent, through leaves.

I am grass near the shore.
Firmly rooted, green,
swept over by your wave,

I bear the dew you leave behind.